NOLLYWOOD

NOLLYWOOD

PIETER HUGO

With texts by

CHRIS ABANI

STACY HARDY

ZINA SARO-WIWA

Prestel
MUNICH · BERLIN · LONDON · NEW YORK

NOLLYWOOD

OMAR SHARIF COMES TO NOLLYWOOD
A STORYBOARD IN 10 FRAMES

CHRIS ABANI

Frame 1:

Establishing shot: small town in Nigeria. 1972. Camera pans through shot. It is a night scene, a dusty motor-park. It is on the south side of the town's market and in the daytime, this is the busiest place in town, the main bus and taxi terminus. Now at night, the cars and buses are parked close together like tombstones. On the white washed wall of the fish market a film is being projected. The space between the parked vehicles and the wall, about sixty feet wide, is packed with the audience who are sitting or standing in front of the makeshift screen. A bunch of children sit on the roof of a lorry parked in the shadows. Before the film begins, a few men with the film company toss cartons of cigarettes into the crowd. A kid at the front catches one and runs it to the lorry. Climbing up, he divides the cigarettes among the cluster of kids aged between seven and eleven. Tonight was a special night; it was double feature night. The last time that happened they had watched a John Wayne double feature. Everyone loved John Wayne. They light up and settle down as the screen comes alive.

On the screen:

A white man is standing in a desert, an Arab pointing a pistol at him. Suddenly a shot rings out, the white man falls to his knees; the Arab falls dead. Another man, on a black horse in black robes and a veiled face rides up. He dismounts, kicks the dead Arab, who looks like him, stoops and picks up his pistol. Slowly the white man comes to his feet as the new Arab removes his veil and speaks: "this is my well", he says. That veiled man was Omar Sharif and his entrance on Lawrence of Arabia **was probably the most dramatic of the last century. To us it was magical and everyone in that dusty motor-park fell in love with Omar Sharif. What a thing, that an African can hold sway on the world stage. Until the double feature —** A Man in the House, **a more obscure Egyptian film. With no subtitles we couldn't understand the dialogue since it was in Arabic, but we knew it was a love story because the musical score mirrored the Hollywood love stories. What was unmistakable were**

the words for God: Allah, inshallah. Two years after the civil war that involved genocide against the predominantly Christian Igbo by the Muslim Hausas, this was a problem. The mood began to change, with every invocation of the Koran or Allah. Everyone loved Omar but soon the crowd went from grumbling to throwing empty beer bottles against the wall until finally two shots rang out — one punched a hole in the wall where Omar's face was, the other killed the already ancient projector.

Frame 2:

Flash-forward: 2006. Hilton Hotel, North Hollywood, LA. First international conference on Nollywood organized by Dr Sylvester Ogbechie of UCSB. Present are scholars, critics, a Cameroonian director, Hollywood folk, mostly from Forest Whitaker and Danny Glover's production companies, some black actors, a Nollywood contingent of directors, writers and actors.

Shot 1:

Panel Discussion — Q and A for directors:

Cameroonian director: **(paraphrasing) I don't even know why I am here talking about the "art" of Nigerian cinema. This is like a Nobel Prize-winning author on a panel with Stephen King talking about "art."**

Nigerian director: **(quote) I understand why my Francophone friend here is jealous of Nollywood. We sell films, lots of films, without any funds from the EU. People never see his movies, but ours are bestsellers within days. The last Francophone "art" film I saw showed a ten-minute shot of a camel standing in a desert doing nothing, not even shitting. I may not know what art is, but this is not it.**

Moderator: **(paraphrasing) Gentlemen, please.**

Shot 2:

A Nigerian director speaks in response to all the critical papers presented on Nollywood. Curiously his accent becomes very thick as he speaks, his syntax changing from the very educated American accented English he communicated with over lunch. I wonder absently if this is some performance like gangsta rap. This is recreated from notes and memory.

Let me begin with a statement, for those of you not knowing, Nollywood is the name of the Nigerian film industry. We call it Nollywood because it is third in money and quantity in the world behind Hollywood and Bollywood only. Let me also state that I appreciate all your essays, very intelligent intellectual ramblings and invocations, but now I will give you the really truth about it. First we begin with motivation, that is when the eureka moment occurs and you say to yourself, or even you sitting in the audience, although here I am talking about myself, so you say, I am going to make a movie. Then you approach Alhaji, this may or may not be a Hausa currency dealer at the airport, it can also be a Nigerian of any tribe and money-making ability, but essentially a person

who can bankroll this film you are about to embark on the production of. As you know, you have to be rich in Nigeria to become an Alhaji, so the richness is the key. Unlike US producers, Alhaji, which by now you can guess is just the term of the bankroller and not a statement of the person's true reality, will give you the money, usually $15,000 max for the loan term of no more than two months and a 30% interest rate. Anyway, you call a writer, in this case his name is Sonny and you say: "Sonny I want a script, Alhaji gave me 10,000 and I need to shoot and wrap to CD/DVD in a week." Then Sonny will say, "what kind of script?" And I say, "Sonny you are the expert, all I need is car crash, a coffin and a vampire or ghost — these I need for suspense and action — the rest is up to you. But I need it in two days, I can pay you 500." Then Sonny will say okay. Then I call someone like Bond Emeruwa who has good cameras, Sony and I will say "Bond we need to shoot between the 23rd and the 26th, can I use your cameras? No crew, maybe one cameraman because my brother John is good on camera also and my DP, Ola, can operate lights." Then I will negotiate a good price with Bond who is very generous to those of us up-and-coming. Next I will call an actress and ask if she is free on a certain day... On the day we were filming the car crash, the police came and chased us. We all helped to carry equipment and run from 3rd mainland bridge, even the actors. Then later that day, my DP and I were fortunate enough to witness a molue bus crashing on the bridge, falling over the side. By the grace of God we had a camera and captured it on film. This is the life of a Nollywood director. Careful planning, and luck...

This goes on for twenty minutes. The audience of Nigerians try hard not to make their laughter obvious, while the Americans "oh" and "ah" at this. Phrases like "real guerrilla filmmaking" are uttered and they bemoan the fact that they may never experience this.

Frame 3:   Exterior shot. Primary school. A knot of kids gathers around two who are facing off in a fight. In the back of the group, bets are being made on the winner and loser.

In my primary school in the small Eastern Nigerian town of Afikpo, there were at least ten boys with the nickname: Omar Sharif. Frequent fights broke out to establish who was the original Omar Sharif and not the Taiwan Omar, Taiwan being the term for interior products. One boy, John, a former boy soldier slowly beat and threatened his way to the top over three weeks. We were all a little upset when he emerged as The Original Omar Sharif or Original Omar because the fights were great entertainment for us after school. By the end of the month in which we had seen that Lawrence of Arabia and the real Omar Sharif had been nicknamed Omar Sharif the Savior of the White Man, there was one Original Omar in my school, but nine variations including Small Omar, Omar the terrible, Omar the Magic Man and Omar Prince of thieves.

Frame 4:   Exterior shot of motor-park terminus. On a dwarf wall, a group of kids drink Coca-Cola and share cigarettes. They are singing in phonetic Hindi, a song learned from a Bollywood movie. They mimic the hand movements and head bobbing. A passing group of adults stop for a while to watch. When the kids falter in their Hindi, they substitute an Igbo word. Seamlessly; naturally.

My favourite Bollywood film was Amar. **Perhaps it was the opening shots with Sonia the milkmaid doing the chores — feeding chickens, sweeping the yard, milking the cow and talking to the animals — these mirrored the rural life we lived; even if, as in my case, we grew up with maids to do these chores. There was the funny scene where Sonia ties a calf to her wicked stepmother's bedpost then chases the calf, which dragged the poor woman about waking her very rudely. Of course all the young boys had a crush on Sonia played by the beautiful Nimmi. In retrospect there was something very Snow White about Sonia and very Disney about the shots — Sonia talks to animals in the early morning mist, birds flock to her when she offers puja, other birds land on her as she skips over the river's stepping stones to fetch water, all the while singing and smiling like Maria von Trap in** The Sound of Music. **All that must have created in us an immediate sense of nostalgia even though we lived the life being mirrored at us. It makes sense, I suppose, that we loved that our lives were romanticized on screen. This kind of personal magic, added to the supernatural play (something we believed in completely) made Bollywood and the early martial arts movies triumph over Hollywood in our hearts. Sonia's looks made her a perfect stand-in for Mami-Wata in the audience's imagination. Mami-Wata, a sometimes benevolent, sometimes malevolent, sometimes human deity was a recent goddess in the Igbo pantheon having been adopted from Riverine and Delta neighbours. Her form, that of a beautiful light-skinned woman with long hair and foreign looks might have come from a ship's masthead that washed up on shore but she matched the Indian women of Bollywood movies perfectly. But what intrigued me most about the movie** Amar **and what set it apart from the other Bollywood movies like** Nagim the Snake Girl, **were the surreal shots that peppered it.**

Frame 5:   Cut to director and DOP talking about how to create the best shot to illuminate the interiority not only of the landscape, but also of the cultural landscape.

The one marker of the Nigerian personality that individuates it from the rest of Africa is the ability to insert its imagined self into the heart of every narrative it receives. Not that other cultures don't do this, but the Nigerian imagination does it so completely and seamlessly that it is quite breathtaking.

When the Blaxploitation movies came out in the seventies, urban Nigerians dressed like pimps in faux fur and velvet suits and hats in

100-degree humidity and they referred to their girlfriends as bitches (pronounced "beeches") with a naivety absent from the original context. The music of James Brown was absorbed by local bands like The Geraldo Pino Funkadeliks, who infused the funk with a little Afro-beat and Highlife. Western TV shows dominated the air, and Hollywood, Bollywood and the Hong Kong Martial Arts industry ruled the cinema — although the word cinema refers to the genre rather than any movie theatres as these were few and far between. Open parks and half torn bed sheets, or the walls of tall buildings next to open lots a crude variation of drive-ins, were the main venues.

Locally made television shows, were for the most part, strange and surreal throwbacks to a pre-colonial identity, or the subversion of a colonial identity and colonialism itself. The danger of proclaiming anything but a common Nigerian identity (a concept that is still new even now since the country is only 45 years old) was a hold over from the civil war.

The only time ethnicity was played up was in straight up comedies and satires like Icheku, the Village Headmaster or Hotel de Jordan. The only things that were never mediated in these shows were the corruption of power, the hypocrisy of religion, the dangers of human sacrifice in animist religions (although there is no evidence this was a pre-colonial practice, religious propaganda suggested that it had been and that only colonial intervention had stopped it) and the plight of the poor. This meant that these shows were often cancelled due to "technical difficulties." Hotel de Jordan was always under threat because even their theme song was controversial — its chorus was: Poor man dey suffer, monkey dey work, baboon dey chop — and was a common anthem of civil servants who would belt it out almost in unison. At 2.30pm, half an hour from the end of the workday, this song could be heard coming from nearly every government building. All these sitcoms borrowed ideas, shots, costume and even class values from American and British TV shows. There was even a children's show about a pet tortoise that saved people. We loved it even though the actor who wore the costume and played the tortoise was nearly six feet tall, and the fact that no one had a pet tortoise as they were considered witch's familiars. This show was modelled on the Australian show — Skippy the Bush Kangaroo.

Frame 6:   Panning shot of Onitsha Market — open air — sprawling, it is perhaps the biggest market in West Africa and has been for years. The shot zooms in to a small bar restaurant locally called a Mama Put. A sign outside reads: Rice and Beans sold here. Also food is ready. The shot is a close up of two men talking.

M1: So this is the heart of Nollywood?
M2: Of course yes, it is. Onitsha is the heart of all the country's intelligent design.
M1: How are you connected to Nollywood?
M2: Well, this is where most of the movies are made, shot, edited,

sold, conceived and so forth. There may be a new generation running things but we started it all with the Onitsha Market Literature. You know? Even, myself, JC Anorue, was a big player in this. My book, The Complete Story and Trail of Adolf Hitler was a bestseller. Now we are like consultants to the new generation. The truth is, we know what sells and how to sell it. Look, I will get more drinks and we will talk more.

As M2, gets up to go fetch more drinks, M1 picks up the pamphlet about *Hitler* and flips through it. He makes one note: if this book is representative of Onitsha Market Literature, then it seems that at its core is the notion of reinvention, retelling and re-rendering of history, cliché and urban legend. He scratches the note out and writes: to hard to sum up in one thought.

M2: (returning to the table) **The drinks are hot here, let's go somewhere else.**

Frame 7:
Interior shot in bar. Several guys are drunk and arguing about the merits of John Wayne versus Actor and who they would rather be. This is a volatile conversation about morals and ethics.

When we watched Westerns as kids in the 1970s, most of them came without sound tracks, and a guy on a megaphone, often very drunk would provide the narrative. The movies were broken down into a simple easy to remember archetypal play: the good guy was always John Wayne (regardless of whom the actor was) and the bad guy was always called Actor. Predictably most of us loved Actor because he lived a dangerous and often ambiguous life. He was always part hero part villain and often the more compelling actor on screen. Omar Sharif became a legend for us when he and Gregory Peck (playing a character called McKenna, but to us "John Wayne") battled in a movie called McKenna's Gold. It was one thing to be the white man's saviour in Lawrence of Arabia, but to become Actor? That for us was the epitome of it all.

Frame 8:
Hilton Hotel, LA. 2006. First Nollywood International Conference. A professor at the podium is delivering a paper.

Nollywood had an already built in and very sophisticated viewership, people who could imaginatively occupy all and any of the roles shown to them, but who at the same time could not always make the distinction between what was real and what was imagined.

Frame 9:
Interior shot of an empty classroom. An audience is gathered at one end, crowded in among the desks and chairs. The other end is a "stage" and a concert is playing out.

This one is called The Man of God Defeats the Forces of Darkness with Nothing but Prayer and A Clean Life — featuring Chief Mike, the best actor as the Pastor.

The other aspect of the local imagination that has really fuelled the "look" of Nollywood were the "concerts." Concerts were morality plays with very simple plot lines about the battle between good and evil, usually cast against class disparity (with the rich characters being evil and usually having their comeuppance at the end. They used a lot of supernatural elements — human sacrifice, ghosts, spirits, vampires — and an emphasis on paybacks. Their portrayal of the supernatural is what is interesting to me. There is an emphasis not on the monster or even freak, but on the grotesque human form. As a writer who employs this idea of the grotesque in my work, I have learned to separate from the simple impulse of "the gross" and "the disgusting." Slasher movies employ the disgusting as opposed to the grotesque. The idea of the grotesque as used in concert is understood and employed well by Japanese films, for instance. It is often the subtle manipulation of the human form to destroy the usual perspective and to move things just slightly off kilter. The grotesque engenders sympathy, revulsion and real fear simply by employing self-recognition with a little displacement. So the body of an actor is sometimes fully nude, painted a deep black or intense white all over, and then the actor employs odd physicality's like walking on his/her hands, crawling like an animal or even just employing silence with a focused open-eyes stare. Although everything so far discussed demonstrates that Nollywood and its antecedents reflected an intense religious and political bent, the aesthetics of the grotesque are mostly at the heart of it. The grotesque always signal carnival, which signals the subversive. So it would seem that at its heart, the aesthetics of Nollywood are set up to subvert the status quo making it intrinsically political. Carnival however, while subverting the status quo necessarily recreates thus simultaneously reinforcing it.

Frame 10: Chris Abani and Bond Emeruwa sit in a bar at the Ngorodo Mountain Lodge in Arusha, Tanzania. It is night and the bar is all but deserted.

Before Nollywood took off, the television soap opera, Cockcrow at Dawn, signalled that there was a shift in the visual narrative of the country. However, it is undeniable that Bond Emeruwa's Living in Bondage began the Nollywood phenomenon and that he is one of the most gifted directors in the fledgling industry. Over late night drinks in a bar in Arusha, Tanzania, Bond and I talked about our influences as artists and the films from our childhood. We talked about the early films of Herbert Ogunde (all in Yoruba which he understood and I didn't), also Ogunde's plays, the Shaolin movies, Jackie Chan in Snake in the Monkey's Shadow, Bruce Lee's Enter the Dragon, Lawrence of Arabia, Alec Guinness and

David Bowie in Bridge Over the River Kwai. **There was also** The Great Escape, Papillion, The Ten Commandments, The Sound of Music, The Good, the Bad and the Ugly, Planet of the Apes **and so on. When I asked Bond about his favourite James Bond movie moment, he sighed and said, when Omar Sharif is a gambler. I remember this scene too, although when I wrote this text, I could find no reference under any of the names Omar used that he had ever been in a James Bond movie. I wonder if it's the Nigerian imagination at work? We both remembered him in** Dr Zhivago **though. That night, I confessed to Bond something I've never told anyone before: I secretly called myself Omar the Gentleman for years.**

NO GOING BACK

ZINA SARO-WIWA

It was at the start of the millennium when I first began encountering what, for me, was a new type of street iconography. They were declamatory, melodramatic posters that had been plastered onto the alleyways and brick walls of inner-city London. Flyposters that demanded attention as they jostled for space amidst faded adverts for club nights and black haircare products. But these posters, the ones that made me stop and stare, told a story. Each one featured a collision of faces. Snapshots of actors, mid-performance, collaged together. Despairing wives clutched their heads, eyeballs upturned to the skies, imploring God for mercy. Devious Jezebels crouched at the bottom of the posters sporting engine-red Afro wigs and long blonde weaves. Alarming nails and make-up. Ogas in traditional West African attire looked harassed. Businessmen in sharp suits checked the time on expensive watches. Time to meet their mistress? Or time to stab their partner in the back, perhaps? These images often made me laugh but were impossible to dismiss or ignore. I knew nothing of their world but I imagined it to be one of outrage, betrayal, revenge and comedy. A land of devious charlatans, saintly wives, suspect businessmen, scheming mistresses, embattled priests and demonic African spirits. Sturm und Drang pantomime. Extreme soap. I did not know it at the time, but I had been stumbling across posters for the Nigerian video film industry. An industry that was writing itself onto the streets and into the consciousness of people in Nigeria, Africa and the diaspora.

Boasting an estimated $320,000,000 annual turnover, Nollywood is often claimed to be the third largest film industry in the world after Hollywood and Bollywood. In terms of volume of output it is likely the most prolific film industry in the world with something in the region 1,000–1,500 films being churned out annually. Birthed in Nigeria, Nollywood has erupted into an African cinematic landscape that had hitherto been dominated — at least in the popular realm — by Hollywood, Bollywood and kung fu movies. But Nollywood is the first time a truly popular indigenous cinematic culture has taken hold and, in many cases, supplanted ordinary Africans' taste for foreign films.

Of course there is an existing indigenous cinema of sub-Saharan Africa. It is a cinema characteristically defined by the films made by Francophone West African directors trained in Europe and the Soviet Union in the 60s and 70s. Typically shot on 35mm, financially-backed by the French Ministry of Co-operation & Development (now Ministry of Foreign Affairs) and other European bodies, Francophone African films are, stereotypically, introspective meditations on postcolonial identity. A cinematic forum where political and ideological concerns are contemplated seriously. Enveloped in moody silence, the stark Sahelian landscapes in these celluloid tales from Senegal, Mali and Burkina Faso, (1) become a visual metaphor for all manner of sublimated social and political ideas. And although this is a cinema funded principally by European bodies, the pursuit of an "authentically African" visual language is assiduously pursued. But these art house offerings find only small audiences at film festivals, embassies and universities. Sometimes referred to caustically as "Embassy Films", they are rarely seen by the majority of so-called ordinary Africans.

(1) *Nollywood in Lagos, Lagos in Nollywood Films* by Jonathan Haynes Vol 54, No 2, 2007

Nollywood could not be more different. If Francophone films prize art and ideas over entertainment, Nollywood's concerns are the inverse. The industry provides low-budget African-authored entertainment that is accessible to all strata of Nigerian and African society. And because Africans are buying these films in their millions, Nollywood has become a financially self-sustaining industry that does not rely on government bodies or European institutions for financing. The films are wordy, improvised, melodramatic morality tales that are often set in shamelessly upwardly-mobile urban Nigerian environments. They are shot on cheap digital technology which has enabled a freewheeling approach to film-making that heavy, expensive 35mm equipment does not allow. These are films made in a hurry. Entire features are shot, cut, packaged and shipped to market in an average of two weeks at a cost of only $10,000 to $50,000. They are not aesthetically beautiful and directors make little attempt at being artistic or subscribing to an intellectual or political agenda. In Nollywood plot and commerce rule. And yet this "authentically African cinema language", beloved of 35mm Francophone African auteurs, is nevertheless achieved. Some images may have been influenced by Western cinema or Bollywood, but Nollywood is encoded with popular mythologies and local concerns. Moreover the hectic and unpredictable Nigerian environment compounded by the necessarily low cost and speed of each film's delivery have, inadvertently, created an aesthetic of circumstance that is uniquely Nollywood.

Although referred to as "movies", Nollywood films borrow more from TV soap opera in terms of visual style and subject matter. In a sense Nollywood films are the soap operas that should have been churned out weekly on TV but have instead been forced out into the open market to fend for themselves, due to an unfavourable industry environment. Natural selection has seen them mutate into a B-movie species adapted to and employing small-screen conventions. For example, films are often split over two, sometimes four, DVDs making each film feel like (feature-length) soap episodes. The incidental music tends to consist of dissonant chords and soundscapes produced on synthesisers, reminiscent of the Latin American telenovelas that are still popular in Nigeria. The films are full of indulgent and interminable soap opera close-ups, all the better to see the tears streaming down people's faces, forcing the viewer to confront the emotions generated by invariably melodramatic plots. Emotions run high in Nollywood and "good acting" appears to be directly correlated to how loud actors can shout and the intensity of pain they perform. The films' sensationalist titles attest to this intemperate humour: Blood Sisters; Beyond Desire; Living in Bondage; Testimonies of Pain; Deadly Desire; Kingdom Against Kingdom; Dangerous Mother; God, Where are You?

But whilst Hollywood and Bollywood films are destined, initially at least, for the big screen, Nollywood films nearly never see the inside of a cinema. Nollywood is a straight-to-DVD industry as there are few multiplexes in Nigeria (cinemas were converted to churches or warehouses in the 80s) and poverty and security issues have militated against a public and communal movie-watching experience. Consequently these films are consumed principally at home but also on public buses and in tiny video parlours that are found on street corners in Nigerian cities and patronised mostly by slum dwellers. But the audience can also be found far beyond Nigeria's borders. Around 600,000 VCDs are pressed daily in Lagos and crates of these films leave on planes everyday for destinations all over Africa (2) making Nigeria one of the leading digital media content producers and Nollywood films one of Nigeria's most important exports after oil. Nollywood films are on TV in Namibia and are on sale on the streets of Nairobi. In Congo, they are broadcast with the soundtrack turned down while an interpreter tells the story in Lingala (3). You can easily access Nollywood films beyond African shores. Wherever there are Africans in the West one will find Nollywood films, often in corner shops selling African goods and in "ethnic" marketplaces. Indeed these films are readily available in anyone's home on dedicated satellite channels and on YouTube. And it isn't just Africans watching these films: Caribbeans, African-Americans and reputedly Chinese people have caught the Nollywood bug. Nollywood may not yet have the profile of Hollywood or Bollywood but its addictiveness has seen it seep deeply into the global digital landscape.

Video films are made all over Nigeria but there are three main centres of production: Lagos, Enugu and Kano. Lagos, a chaotic, sprawling

(2) *Report on Nollywood Rising Conference* by Brian Larkin, 2005

(3) *Nollywood: What's in a Name?* By Jonathan Haynes (Film International, 2007)

metropolis of at least an estimated 8 (some say 15) million people is Nollywood's premiere production site, followed by Enugu a smaller city in the south-east of Nigeria. The films emanating from Kano in the predominantly Muslim north of Nigeria plead a separate identity and monicker: "Kanywood". Kanywood movies are more folkloric and take their cue from Bollywood featuring song and dance numbers sung in Hausa and Arabic (though there is not the same level of spectacle). But the movies that travel the furthest and, to some extent, define the genre are the English-language films that come from the south of the country where the boom began.

The first Nollywood film was produced by a Lagos-based businessman named Kenneth Nnebue. He was, reputedly, having trouble selling a consignment of blank VHS tapes from Taiwan and thought he might shift the tapes quicker if there were something on them. Inspired by an existing informal film industry that consisted of amateur VHS recordings of the performances of Yoruba theatre troupes and also, perhaps, inspired by the existence of a nascent Ghanaian video film industry, Nnebue decided to have a go at making a video himself. His first film titled Living in Bondage was released in two parts in 1992 and sold an unprecedented 500,000 copies.

In retrospect it comes as no surprise that Living in Bondage was so popular. Nigeria was being sold a (sensationalist) story of her own modern urban reality, packaged seductively in the same cellophane-wrapped manner of imported movies. Furthermore the plot truly spoke to Nigerians: Andy, the protagonist, eager to make it in the city of Lagos, gets sucked into a cult that demands the ritual sacrifice of his wife in exchange for riches. He eventually makes his millions only to be haunted by the ghost of his wife. Ultimately, he seeks and finds salvation in the church. The horror of ritual murder, the fall into vice and the redemption provided by Christ are all themes that resonate in a society with great inequality of wealth. For although one of the largest oil producers in the world, Nigeria's economic growth and rapid urbanisation has not been accompanied by a decline in unemployment or poverty. Indeed over half the population still live on a dollar a day. In addition, inept, kleptomaniac rulers have sown an atmosphere of frustration, desperation and corruption resulting in an ingrained disbelief in the possibility of an ethical order. For this reason the pursuit of money and status and the role of supernatural forces within this chaos provide potently resonant narratives.

The pre-dominant focus on the urban experience is perhaps the subliminal captivating factor of Nollywood. Urbanisation is Africa's biggest macro-economic and socio-political drama, the great untold story of the continent. The foreign media focus primarily on rural

(4) *Urbanization and Insecurity in West Africa Population Movements, Mega Cities and Regional Stability*, Unowa Issue Papers, October, 2007

(5) *State of African Cities Report 2008* by Un-Habitat

(6) *The State of the World's Cities 2004/2005* by United Nations Human Settlements Programme

poverty and have little-to-no sense of African urban culture. EU-funded Francophone African film-makers have been forced to display a similar myopia as the overall funding criteria and subject matter for their films have been determined by their European benefactors who broadly deem urban Africa "inauthentically" African and rural Africa "pure" or "untainted". Africa now has the highest rate of urban growth in the world (4.4% against a global average of 2.5%) (4) and will enter its urban age in 2030 with around 760 million people — half of its total population — living in cities (5). Indeed Lagos is reputedly on course to becoming the third largest city in the world by 2015 (6). The city is inventing Africa and Nollywood is one of the few industries providing narratives that navigate this radical, ongoing shift.

It is no surprise then that Nollywood is, for the most part, an urbane and aspirational televisual culture whose principle theatres of action are the homes, offices and universities of Nigeria's urban middle classes. (Some would say that to be "authentically" Nigerian is to be aspirational). It is within these, sometimes opulent, walls that popular urban romances and family melodramas unfold. (Nollywood stories are rarely about federal politics. The politics is local, moral and emotional). In Beyonce & Rihanna, for example, the two female protagonists vie for the attention of music producer Jay Jay in his palatial home as well as in African Idol-style singing contests. Who will he choose? Love and hate is also explored in family melodramas. In Caught in the Act 1 and 2, a woman (played by Nollywood's premiere actress Genevieve Nnaji) is wrongly accused of abducting her own child and is sentenced to death whilst the over-possessive mother-in-law (resplendent in burgundy painted eyebrows, flamboyant clothing and terrifying glare) delights in her daughter-in-law's fate as it allows her to maintain a close relationship with her son. It is in fact the daughter-in-law's long-lost twin sister (also played by Nnaji) who has become a prostitute and child trafficker that is behind the abduction.

Human trafficking and prostitution form the meat of the so-called "City Girl" video. Kenneth Nnebue's second film Glamour Girls initiated this genre and was the first video film to address the rise in child-trafficking and prostitution amongst young, even middle-class Nigerian females. In the film four innocent girlfriends are lured unknowingly into prostitution. All end up running their own successful women-trafficking syndicates. But greed and jealousy set in and the women destroy one another. (Women are prominent in Nollywood but suffer from stereotyping. They are the wicked stepmother, the wealthy but predatory urban spinster, the saintly wife, the Madonna or the whore).

The corruption of urban Nigerian life is also explored through gangster movies. Though inspired by Hollywood and kung fu movies, there is little money for major action sequences. But car chases and fights make up for the lack of explosions and hi-tech stunts. A uniquely Nigerian sub genre of the gang movie would be the ones that highlight the "campus cult" phenomenon. Since the 1990s Nigerian universities have found themselves under the grip of gangs or "cults" whose objective is to control the universities and secure good degree results using extortion, robbery and sometimes rape. Films like Campus Queen **and** Campus Lords reflect the rise in this very real terrorism.

The ever-pressing concerns about the moral degeneracy in Nigerian society and the growing role of the church in dealing with the malaise has seen the rise of so-called "hallelujah" movies. The popularity of this category of video film has soared mostly due to the depleting economic resources of many Nigerians who now seek solace [in droves] in the promise of a heavenly polis of bliss and eternal happiness (7). Very often churches themselves will produce such films in a bid to attract larger congregations.

(7) *Women, Religion and the video film in Nigeria* by Onookome Okome (Film International, 2004)

It is not, however, all doom and gloom. Nollywood does a brisk trade in comedy. A prominent strand of these comedies feature the popular duo Chinedu Ikedieze and Osita Iheme (who are adults that suffer from a rare type of dwarfism that makes them look like children) who cause all sorts of mayhem in films like Daddy Must Obey, Reggae Boys **and** Tom and Jerry. And at the start of the industry there was a salacious strand that featured women with extremely large breasts. Farcical storylines were woven around them and their mammaries. The notion of political correctness, you will find, has not troubled Nollywood. But the most popular of all the genres is the "voodoo horror" or "Juju" video. These feature dramas about ritual killings carried out for financial gain and also supernatural thrillers involving spirits, vampires and ghosts. Juju films kicked off the Nollywood industry back in 1992 and have endured. There are many reasons for their popularity but one is tempted to cite the fact that belief in the spirit world is always very close to the surface of Nigerian life despite the firm grip of Christianity and Islam (as a glance at Sunday tabloid papers will attest). The Juju videos visualise what people secretly suspect is always there and provide emotionally-satisfying explanations for wealth inequalities or injustices that abound in Nigeria.

To my mind, the Juju movies provide the most entertaining visual dramas. Occult forces in Nollywood films can appear in highly traditional tribal raffia skirts and face paint. Sometimes the evil forces are represented in a way that seems vampire-like or just downright bizarre. In these cases the costuming and make-up seems more suited to the theatre and wouldn't look out of place on the stage. Despite the amateur dramatics approach to costuming, the aesthetic visualisation of the occult in action draws on science-fiction: knives fly magically through the air and evil spirits fire killer laser beams from bright green eyes. Spirits appear and disappear using basic camera techniques of stopping the camera. The rudimentary special effects appear farcical but are very Nollywood and constitute some of its most memorable and unique sequences.

But not all Nigerians are enamoured with the genre and this focus on the occult has, since the beginning of the industry, inspired anger and opprobrium in Nigeria. Juju films are thought to tarnish Nigeria's image even further and are seen as bad for the nation's moral health. Indeed the industry as a whole presents a paradox: Nigeria is at once fiercely proud and yet utterly ashamed of Nollywood. Proud of the fact that Nollywood is a Nigerian-run global industry but ashamed that the content is so under-contemplated and ashamed that after 20 years the production quality is still so abysmal. Extremely poor sound is a major complaint. Frequent changes in recording levels take place from scene to scene. Sometimes the dialogue is so quiet it is drowned out by the incidental music while at other times the dialogue is recorded so loud the boom microphone buzzes and the sound distorts. The over-simplicity of conflict resolution can be preposterous, unrealistic characterisation alongside a general lack of emotional truth can grate and then there is the terrible dialogue which simply does no justice to the natural lyricism and wit of Nigerians. A scandal for a nation that has produced some of the world's greatest writers and whose oral culture is so rich.

But the perceived thematic and aesthetic limitations of Nollywood become more understandable when you consider the conditions under which Nollywood films are made. Time and budgetary constraints are the biggest problems for Nollywood film-makers. Producers are often not able to finance their films from banks, sponsorship or government loans. Their films are generally financed by the producer/director's pocket or by those marketing the film. A less-than-perfect distribution system and rampant piracy make large investments in single films risky meaning that budgets are kept low at around $20,000 (8). Because the budgets are so low and time is of utmost importance to film-makers using their own money, shooting must be quick. This gives rise to a host of short cuts on the production. Time is also compromised by everyday frustrations of Nigerian life that would test the patience of most non-Nigerians. Power cuts — a several-times-daily occurrence in Nigeria — delay filming and the private generators that kick in when the national grid has failed are so loud it can drown out dialogue making shooting near impossible. Actors working simultaneously on other projects may turn up late. And then there is the traffic — notoriously bad in Lagos — which also makes it difficult for crews to get to the set on time. Where time has been lost, emphasis is placed on moving the plot forwards

(8) *Nollywood in Lagos, Lagos in Nollywood Films* by Jonathan Haynes Vol 54, No 2, 2007

so the script, often minimal in the first place, ends up being improvised as scenes are slashed on the spot. This is film-making at it's most pragmatic.

But, it is argued (vigorously on Nigerian blogs), that many a great film has been made on a small budget without the same basic mistakes. The reason for Nollywood's apparent amateurism is precisely because Nollywood is comprised of untrained amateurs, learning on the job, buoyed not by artistic merit, but sales. Businessmen and marketers trying their luck at the latest method for making a buck. Indeed the stasis — both thematically and aesthetically — of Nollywood is blamed mostly on the marketers of Nollywood movies. Marketers bankroll the movies while the creative personalities who lack the necessary funds are forced to defer to them. Businessmen first and foremost, they make sure they only fund movies they are sure will become commercial successes. These, sometimes illiterate, marketers not only set the theme, budget and delivery date but they also dictate the script and cast. Some marketers have even tried their hand at directing movies. This have-a-go approach is laudable in one sense but has left us with films that can beggar belief in terms of production quality. As veteran Nollywood director Charles Igwe has pointed out: "Our people took a jump off a cliff and landed in the middle of the ocean. Then we started building the boats while we were in the water."

Nollywood breaks many film-making rules and does not often get away with them. But whilst a few of the films are almost unwatchable there are many that are genuinely entertaining on a variety of levels. These films occupy an intriguingly ambiguous realm that is between self-consciousness and naivety. Between the hyper real and the totally unrealistic. The low budget aesthetic (like that other cheap, straight-to-video film industry: the porn industry) invites voyeurism. Like watching couples argue on a street, it feels free of convention, as if anything can happen. And often it does. The plots can be wonderfully involving. Often beginning with a dramatic turn of events: a murder, a room full of children with their mouths taped up, a car-jacking, one is immediately drawn in and one wants to know why and what happens next. The better movies feature genuinely surprising plot twists that leave you watching silently like a child being told an absorbing bedtime story. The poor production becomes a mere detail. And even if you are left spluttering in disbelief at the ending or feel cheated by the unsatisfactory resolution of a conflict you are more than ready to try your luck with another title in the hope of exorcising the last.

There are occasional flashes of brilliance in these films: some of the acting when in the hands of the right director can be very convincing. You can also come across genuinely funny (and not merely inadvertently funny) dialogue. In the historical films I have come across wonderful Yoruba aphorisms that have had me reaching for a pen and paper to scribble them down. And for many Nigerians, part of the joy of watching these films is simply seeing Nigeria reflected back at them. Nigerians in the diaspora often watch these films to learn about what is going on in Nigeria and to provide a cultural connection to children that may have been born and brought up in the West. The subject matter is often taken from newspapers and shoots take place in people's actual homes and offices. In many ways one is truly watching Nigeria.

Nollywood has much to offer but it is currently an industry in peril: revenues are down, costs are rising and fewer films are being made. The arrival of the African movie channel Africa Magic has caused much upset in the industry as it is claimed that they do not pay proper exhibition or royalty fees and people are now able to watch Nollywood movies for free. There is the hope that Nollywood will follow the same evolutionary path as the music video industry. Nigerian music videos were amateurish and of poor quality which hampered the sales of the artists as they were unable to get onto the new African MTV station and Channel O. But as soon as they raised their game, they were able to appear on these channels enabling Nigerian music stars to achieve international recognition. Unless distribution channels can be improved then there is little likelihood a similar shift will happen in Nollywood and the quality of these films will simply never improve. But the mood within the industry is that of impatience with the poor quality so this crisis point may yet beget a new and more interesting phase in the life of Nigerian film.

Nollywood deserves to thrive. For all its failings, this industry provides a vision of Nigeria and Africa that has been wrested from the ideologies of foreign bodies and distributors that want to impose their own vision of Africa. And this is a wonderful and long-overdue turn of events. For the first time and in the purest, rawest form, Africa is representing and interpreting Africa. Nigeria is pumping out her own stories and inspiring other African countries to do the same. Nollywood has allowed Africans to dream in Africa and find release in their own continent. Africans no longer need to worship Jackie Chan, Bruce Willis or Amitabh Bachchan, they can look to their own screen idols: Peter Edochie, Francis Duru or Genevieve Nnaji if they so wish.

And even if you are underwhelmed by the films, the tenacity and sheer guts of the film-makers themselves cannot fail to impress and their work offers up a fascinating and humbling lesson for film-producers the world over who are easily cowed by supposedly trying environments. This story of Nigerian agency encoded in the story of the industry is a powerful and important narrative in itself for Nigeria and Africa. In a country where the petroleum-led economy has made trillions yet has improved scandalously few lives, Nollywood has allowed Nigerians, Africans and the world to observe an African-led industry offer creativity, remuneration, community development and even stardom to anyone with flair and an entrepreneurial spirit. It is a phenomenon with powerful implications for the cultural and ultimately economic development of Africa.

References:

Nollywood in Lagos, Lagos in Nollywood Films by Jonathan Haynes (Indiana University Press, 2007)
Introducing the Special Issue on West African Cinema: Africa at the Movies by Onookome Okome (Film International, 2007)
Women, Religion and the Video Film in Nigeria by Onookome Okome (Film International, 2004)
Interviews with Amaka Igwe, Tunde Kelani and Kenneth Nnebue by Uzoma Esonwanne (Research in African Literatures, Indiana University Press, 2008)

Videography:

Beyonce & Rihanna 1–4, dir. Afam Okereke
Kingdom Against Kingdom 1 & 2, dir. Ugo Ugbor
Akinko, dir. Sylvester Ogbolu
Tom & Jerry, dir. Kenneth Egbuna
Caught in the Act 1 & 2, dir. Charles Inojie
Blood Sister 1 & 2, dir. Chidi Chikere
Peace Mission, dir. Dorothee Wenner
Welcome to Nollywood, dir. Jamie Meltzer
A Brief History of Nollywood, dir. Awam Amkpa

Acknowledgements:

Mahen Bonetti, New York African Film Festival
Ben Lampert, Department of Geography, UCL
Dr. Awam Amkpa, Director of African Studies, NYU

NOLLYWOOD CONFIDENTIAL

STACY HARDY

Horror for me started at age 13 with vampires. Not the classic kind. Not Dracula or even Fright Night but Rabid, David Cronenberg's feverish early sci-fi horror porn. I remember the fear. Hands, little fists clutching the remote control, fingers itching, twitchy. I remember that feeling. The dizzy swell of skin making sweat, eyes swimming in their sockets, the thrill of watching what I wasn't allowed to watch: someone losing their mind, someone growing claws and hair, someone naked, panting, someone sucking a woman's neck with their fangs.

Mostly I remember the blood: too red. The fadeout on the heroine's body: her face larger than the frame; uncontrollable lust, eyes that bleed beyond the screen. I don't remember the plot, the story. I do remember I returned the tape unwound.

Fast forward. Flicking through Pieter Hugo's Nollywood series is like a rewind. I'm banged back.

The vampire bent over the corpse. Eyes that shine like polished copper. The lips draw back as the mouth opens. The teeth are exposed.

The monster so close you could touch it. I want to look away but I can't. I'm sucked in; the thrill and of being too close to things, the fear of seeing how close I could get, of seeing what I wasn't allowed to see. My eyes. Something pushing from the inside out. I look and look. Like the reconditioning finale in A Clockwork Orange, where Alex's eyes are pried open with metal spiders so that the movies can slip in like ghosts, like vampires.

Part of the discomfort is the politics. Isn't this stuff meant to be exploitative? I'm thinking of Marx's famous description of capital: "dead labour which, vampire-like, lives only by sucking living labour, and lives the more, the more labour it sucks." Colonial vampire: bloodsucking foreigner draining the lifeblood out of Africa. The monster that wont die, seducing its victim into erotically charged feeding frenzies of capitalist extraction. Its victims thus infected, colonised, by the vampiric impulse. The endless cycle.

It's all so easy to blame history. To theorise my discomfort, put the words on the page between me and the pictures. Write them off. To disarm my fear. But that's just a part of the story. Something else haunts me: something much messier, thicker, much redder, too red...

My eyes are locked on the images but my mind drifts back to the cyber 90s. Donna Haraway had this theory: she initiated us into the vampire's rituals of blood. She saw the vampire as a transgressive figure, infecting blood; threatening normal human constructs with racial and sexual mixing.

It's like this: if the obsession with strictly defined boundaries haunts Western conceptions of subjectivity, perhaps the vampire, the figure who lives by crossing lines, messing with those boundaries tells us something about how they are made, how they can be ripped down.

The bloodsucker caught in the act, lips draw back from his teeth, the glow that emerges from deep within his eyes.

With incisive detachment and rampant imagination, he feeds, transferring an illegitimate substance, transforming his "victims" from the living to the undead, giving birth without sex, trafficking in the unruly logics of fluids, mixing and spilling and infecting blood.

Boundaries become confused: documentary bleeds into fiction as reality and fantasy fuse. Nollywood and Hollywood trade secrets. Catwomen of Outer Space-style sci-fi mixes with Black Caesar-style syncretic Blaxploitation. Spiritual belief systems are played through videogame warzone in an unlicensed gameshow-without-end. Identity changes and shifts and cracks open. As Haraway writes, the vampire "drinks and infuses blood in a paradigmatic act of infecting whatever poses as pure."

The Madonna reimaged as the ghost of the Emperor Haile Selassie meets Idi Amin, *Charlie's Angels* do *Rambo* — *Foxy Brown*-style, David Lynch's *Lost Highway* snakes through Lagos, Ghostface Killa mutates into Fela's "Zombie" and Dracula gives way for Blacula. Voodoo, hoodoo and mambo are mashed up with Igbo rituals. Ahhwooooo... The werewolves of Lagos.

Time is stretched/reversed/accelerated — fu(n)cked-up. In The Land of 1000 Demons bodies rise from the rumble like the gyrating undead child soldiers in Emmauel Dongal's Johnny Mad Dog. Landscapes that recall T.S. Eliot's Wasteland (itself a blasted stretch made up of dead fragments including

Bram Stoker's Dracula) are remixed with Public Enemy's crack-hammered badlands and CNN-style hell-on-Earth war zones.

Soldiers garbed in camouflage uniforms, festooned with weaponry: pistols, hand grenades, dangling rifles. Bloody limbs strewn about the floor, a body dismembered.

It's all happening now. Philosophising vampires, Deleuze and Guattari tell us: "We live today in the age of partial objects, bricks that have been shattered to bits, and leftovers." Here fragments and ruins are no longer melancholy reminders of a vanished order. They've become instead the pieces of a hyperactive child's playground.

The play continues as Hugo inserts himself in the mix via a self-portrait of the photographer as a young colonial blood-sucker, the hooded (in the hood?) white slave-trader/executioner. His self-conscious meta-commentary is upended, unmasked by a reverse mirror image, an inverted photographic negative featuring a black alter-ego, a cold and forbidding, more-than-masculine naked gimp; an oversized dick with a Darth Vader death-head.

Through this double-play Hugo assaults divisions — white vs black, dominant vs submissive, author vs authority, Alien vs Predator, Ekwensu vs God — simultaneously embracing the worst stereotypes and snarling "fuck you" at all of them. The result is something akin to that which happened when Afrika Bambaataa dropped the melody from Kraftwerk's Trans Europe Express into Soul Sonic Force's Planet Rock. Rhythmic bursts. Like blood thudding in the ears. Not so much a deconstruction as a calculated destruction of representation itself. Features cut loose from their trajectory/presence in time, red stains wrecking physiology. I watch the red spread. I feel my face flush.

Welcome To the Terrordome. And Nollywood is scary shit, but not in a Holly-wood way. Rather than employ the rituals of history, myth and mystery to seduce and then placate us, scare it all away — all the shit that's not suppose to be scary but really is — Pieter Hugo throws it in our face.

A dagger through the heart. The bodice ripped wide open. The loose breasts roll.

According to Baudrillard seduction is "that which lets appearance circulate and move as a secret"; it "makes things appear and disappear." Monsters are seductive, therefore, because they are never wholly present; they allure my gaze, beyond visibility, into the realm of that which is secret and hidden. The West is transfixed by the media's negative portrayal of Africa, what's been called its "horror index" precisely because it invents a "pathology of spectrality and transience."

In opposition to this, Hugo's monsters confront us on their own terms; head on, they stare us down. Instead of lurking in the shadows or hiding under the bed of our eternal subconscious nightmare, the figures are starkly light. Their bodies undo sight. Monsters from a nation's Id suddenly demanding equal time as thinking and dreaming and sexual citizens. They face us without even the faintest glimmer of a possible absence, in the state of radical disillusion; Baudrillard's "obscene transparency" of "pure presence."

What Nollywood seems to be suggesting is that it is not the "I" of the photographer or even the "I" of the viewer, but the eye of the camera. We're thrown from "representation" (of something real) to "simulation" (with no secure reference to reality), the normal relation between sign and referent radically remixed so that we lose the connection, once presumed to exist, between sign or image and the reality to which both were thought to refer.

It's an "unfamiliar" unconscious, a hyper-real d(r)ead zone, a different primal scene, one that does grow out of the old dramas of identity and reproduction. Not nation but a radical Alien Nation. Hugo's work occupies that edge, the t(r)ipping point where narrative turns into an endless cycle of rejecting, appropriating and expelling, digressing from the thread of the possible, to the impossible. The radical otherness evoked by the images opens up an outside, a displacement of the deadlock of cynical capital power we find ourselves in; the possibility of other worlds without the trivial categories and opposites within Earthly language.

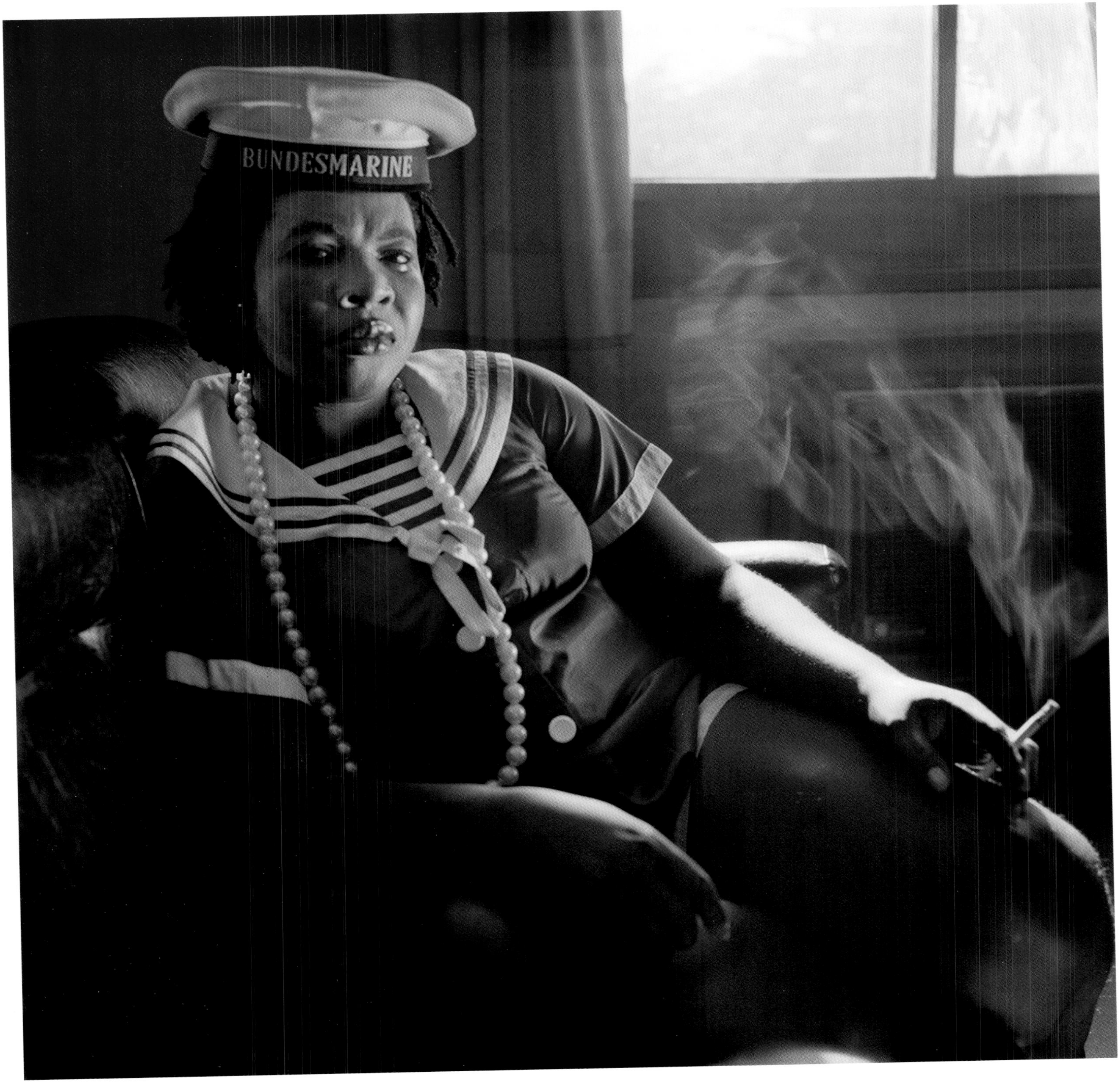
BUNDESMARINE

THIS BOOK IS DEDICATED TO
GABAZZINI ZUO

Escort Kama
ENUGU, NIGERIA, 2008

John Mark
ASABA, NIGERIA, 2008

Emeka Uzzi
ENUGU, NIGERIA 2009

**Chris Nkulo
and Patience Umeh**
ENUGU, NIGERIA, 2008

Emeka Onu
ENUGU, NIGERIA, 2008

John Dollar Emeka
ENUGU, NIGERIA, 2008

Obechukwu Nwoye
ENUGU, NIGERIA, 2008

Untitled
ENUGU, NIGERIA, 2008

Clinton Ibeto
ENUGU, NIGERIA, 2008

Song Iyke
ENUGU, NIGERIA, 2008

Untitled
ENUGU, NIGERIA, 2008

Gabazzini Zuo
ENUGU, NIGERIA, 2008

Kelechi Nwanyeali
Enugu, Nigeria, 2009

Maureen Obise
Enugu, Nigeria, 2009

Tarry King Ibuzo
Enugu, Nigeria, 2008

Casmiar Onyenwe
Enugu, Nigeria, 2008

**Malachy Udegbunam
with children**
Enugu, Nigeria, 2008

Azuka Adindu
Enugu, Nigeria, 2008

**Junior Ofokansi,
Chetachi Ofokansi,
Mpompo Ofokansi**
Enugu, Nigeria, 2008

Omo Omeonu
Enugu, Nigeria, 2008

Fidelis Elenwa
Enugu, Nigeria 2009

**Emilia Ibeh, Doris Orji
and Sharon Opiah**
Enugu, Nigeria, 2008

Ngozi Oltiri
Enugu, Nigeria, 2009

Ibegbu Natty
Enugu, Nigeria, 2008

Untitled
Enugu, Nigeria, 2008

Untitled
Enugu, Nigeria, 2008

Rose Njoku
Enugu, Nigeria, 2008

**Izunna Onwe
and Uju Mbamalu**
Enugu, Nigeria, 2008

Malachy Udegbunam
Enugu, Nigeria, 2008

**Dike Ngube
and Gold Gabriel**
Enugu, Nigeria, 2008

Princess Adaobi
Enugu, Nigeria, 2008

Thompson
Asaba, Nigeria, 2008

**Chommy Choko Eli,
Florence Owanta,
Kelechi Anwuacha**
Enugu, Nigeria, 2008

**Major Okolo
and Do Somtin**
Enugu, Nigeria, 2008

Untitled
Enugu, Nigeria, 2008

**Song Iyke
with onlookers**
Enugu, Nigeria, 2008

Linus Okereke
Enugu, Nigeria, 2008

Chigozie Nechi
Enugu, Nigeria, 2009

**Chika Onyejekwe,
Junior Ofokansi,
Thomas Okafor**
Enugu, Nigeria, 2009

Pieter Hugo
Enugu, Nigeria 2009

Mr Enblo
Enugu, Nigeria, 2008

ACKNOWLEDGEMENTS

Gabriel Okorie Zuo and his family: Grace, Gold and Angel, Adetokunbo Abiola,
Ifanyi Ololo, Chris Abani, Zina Saro-Wiwa, Stacy Hardy, Michael Stevenson,
Federica Angelucci, Joost Bosland, Andrew da Conceicao, Sophie Perryer,
Yossi Milo, Alissa Schoenfeld, Marloes Krijnen, Colette Olof, Marcel Feil,
Malcolm Smith, Awoiska van der Molen, Wim van Sinderen, Cokkie Snoei,
Guido Schlinkert, Sean O'Hagan, Mark Sealy, Indra Khanna, Patrick Henry,
Mike Berg, Robert Carlisle, Clinton Smith, Aaron Schumann, Michket Krifa,
Chantal Grande, Markus Blank, Thomas Korus, Thomas Unruh, Damien Poulain,
Curt Holtz, Elisabeth Biondi, Shamus Clisset, Bridget Baker, Julia Clark,
Oliver Kruger, Tamsyn Reynolds.

My special thanks to all the actors for their generous assistance and help
with the realization of this project.

CREDITS

© Prestel Verlag, Munich · Berlin · London · New York, 2009
© for images Pieter Hugo, 2009
© for text the authors, 2009

Prestel Verlag
Königinstrasse 9
80539 Munich
Tel +49 (89) 24 29 08-300
Fax +49 (89) 24 29 08-335

Prestel Publishing Ltd.
4 Bloomsbury Place
London WC1A 2QA
Tel +44 (0) 20 7323-5004
Fax +44 (0) 20 7636-8004

Prestel Publishing
900 Broadway, Suite 603
New York, N.Y. 10003
Tel +1 (212) 995-2720
Fax +1 (212) 995-2733

www.prestel.com

Prestel books are available worldwide. Please contact your nearest bookseller
or one of the above addresses for information concerning your local distributor.

Library of Congress Control Number: 2009927197

British Library Cataloguing-in-Publication Data: a catalogue record for this book
is available from the British Library. The Deutsche Bibliothek holds a record of
this publication in the Deutsche Nationalbibliografie; detailed bibliographical data
can be found under: http://dnb.ddb.de

Editorial direction by Curt Holtz
Design and layout by Damien Poulain, London
Origination by Laumont Editions, New York
Production by Nele Krüger
Printed and bound by Passavia Druckservice, Passau

Printed in Germany on acid-free paper

Mixed Sources
Product group from well-managed
forests and other controlled sources
www.fsc.org Cert no. SGS-COC-003859
© 1996 Forest Stewardship Council

ISBN 978-3-7913-4312-9